This book is designed to provide biblical information regarding the subject matter covered. However, it is sold with the understanding that the author and publisher are not engaged in rendering legal, financial, or other professional advice. Laws and practice often vary from state to state, and if legal or other expert assistance is required, the services of a professional should be sought. The author and publisher specifically disclaim any and all liability that is incurred from the use or application of the content of this book.

Global Economic Plan for God's People / by Dale S., Jr. – 2nd Ed.

Cover Design by
James E. Walker

Manufactured in the United States
of America

ISBN: 978-1-4675-4157-2

S.I.A. Publishing
1976 S. La Cienega Blvd., Suite 268
Los Angeles, CA 90034
1.888.490.3190

If you are unable to order this book from your local bookseller, you may order directly from the publisher. Special discounts may apply for bulk purchases.

GEPGP™

Global Economic Plan for God's People

"You too can eat the fat of the land."

Dale S., Jr.

S.I.A. Publishing

Acknowledgments

God: Thank You for Your Word, which is life, spirit, and truth. Thank You for giving me the strength to endure this life. Thank You for Your Son, Jesus Christ.

My Family: Wife, I'm grateful to have you as my companion on this journey called life. Mother, I am thankful to have you as my mother. You always pray for me and encourage me to keep going. Dad, the knowledge you have given me over the years has been priceless. You have proven to be a great dad. Pastor T.K. Anderson, you have exemplified the love of Christ as my pastor. Keep up the good works. Grandmother, your words still echo in my mind, "Jr., don't expect nobody to do nothing for you." This statement has pushed me through life and has caused me to be more independent. Thanks!

To my uncle Milton Green, you took time to introduce me to the Word of Faith and made me a ministering prayer warrior. Thank you.

My Friends: Andre Byers, we have been friends for over a decade. You saw something in me that I didn't see in myself and inspired me to move forward. Alfredo Almanza, a man of God, you have always supported my dreams, thoughts, and ideas. Thank you. My dear friend Daron Champion, you made me a fisher of men financially.

Pastor Johnny and Jenice Gentry, thank you both for being loving, caring, and transparent. My life has been changed forever by the "Encounter God Weekend." Keep up the blessed works. Free Indeed Church International, thank you for your love and support. Pam Depass, thank you for all of your prayers and encouragement throughout the years. Boyce Holmes, thank you for all the relationship advice and for always taking the time to listen to me in my times of need. A big special thanks to my Aunt Paula for caring enough to push me to do my best writing works.

Special thanks to all the contributors, readers, staff, family, and friends who supported this effort.

Dedication

This book is dedicated to anyone who has a dream, a vision, and/or a goal, and to those with Faith in Jesus Christ.

In loving memory
of
Mozelle Shepherd
&
Donald Hughes

May your example of love's principles continue to inspire us all to love others as Christ loves the Church.

CONTENTS

Global Economic Plan for God's People

A plan for humanity to implement now, during this time of the mass destruction of our civilization, for the liberation of the people of earth. To create peace on earth, as it is in the heavens, and to restore unity in our communities and abroad. To promote love, life, and goodwill towards all men. To balance the universe with positivity. To empower God's people with the necessary knowledge to survive the genocide on all who love freedom.

1  F.A.T.

Fully Anointed Tabernacle

Exodus 25:8-9 (KJV)

^{8}*And let them make me a sanctuary; that I may dwell among them. ^{9}According to all that I shew thee, after the pattern of the tabernacle, and the pattern of all the instruments thereof, even so shall ye make it.*

God is calling all people to be a tabernacle for Himself. In the Old Testament, the tabernacle was God's dwelling place. Today, God wants to dwell within man. His presence in us is the anointing. The same powerful words God spoke to Moses on how to build His tabernacle is our pattern for today. We are God's holy tabernacle, and as such we are equipped with all of the ingredients needed to produce change on this earth.

Exodus 4:10-12 (AMP)

[10]Then Moses said to the Lord, "Please, Lord, I am not a man of words (eloquent, fluent), neither before nor since you have spoken to

your servant; for I am slow of speech and tongue. [11] The Lord said to him, "Who has made man's mouth? Or who makes the mute or the deaf, or the seeing or the blind? Is it not I, the Lord? [12] Now then go, and I, even I, will be with your mouth, and will teach you what you shall say."

This passage proves that God has already equipped us with all that we need to fulfill His will for our lives. Sometimes we get discouraged or feel inadequate without a relationship with God. That's because we are inadequate without Him. Let me explain. The Holy Scriptures instruct us to make God and His kingdom our highest priority.

Matthew 6:33 (KJV)

33But seek ye first the kingdom of God, and his righteousness; and all these things shall be added unto you.

Numbers 15:39 (AMP)

39It shall be a tassel for you to look at and remember all the commandments of the Lord, to do them, so that you do not follow after (the desires of) your own heart and eyes, (desires) after which you used to follow and play the prostitute.

Wow! As we follow these simple instructions, "seek God first and His righteousness" all the other things we need are automatically added to us: food, shelter, health, and more.

Psalm 37:4 (KJV)

⁴Delight thyself also in the LORD: and he shall give thee the desires of thine heart.

What are your desires? To finish school? Buy your family a home? Have a better relationship with Jesus?

This kind of lifestyle can only be lived by truly putting God first in our lives. God is able to make all grace abound to you and your family in even the toughest of times. I used to try to do everything by my own will and it seemed that life just moved in

a circle. I could never seem to excel.
Now that I have surrendered my will
to God's will, my life has been
excelling with ease.

Matthew 11:30 (KJV)

*30For my yoke is easy, and my burden
is light.*

I have concluded this to be true in my
walk with God. My life has never
been so fulfilling. My brothers and
sisters, if you are looking for a
change from the 9-to-5 mentality, the
hustle and bustle of life, then this
book is for you.

Let's take a look at more of God's promises for those who seek Him first.

Joshua 1:8 (KJV)

⁸This book of the law shall not depart out of thy mouth; but thou shalt meditate therein day and night, that thou mayest observe to do according to all that is written therein: for then thou shalt make thy way prosperous, and then thou shalt have good success.

Did you read that? This passage clearly states that, "…then thou shalt have good success." If there is such a thing as good success there must also be a "bad" success? Could bad success be entertainers we love on

TV flaunting their wealth and riches? Slave labor? The things of this world are carnal so, in most cases, we should question the "goodness" of worldly success. God wants Believers to be a fully anointed tabernacle where He can dwell. He wants our success to be truly "good" just as He is good. Only in God's presence is there fullness of joy and good success.

What Do I Have to Do to Get Started?

It's really simple! To get started all you have to do is follow these 4 simple steps for salvation.

4 Simple Steps:

1. Acknowledge in your heart that Jesus is Lord.

2. Confess with your mouth that Jesus is Lord.

3. Believe that Jesus died for your sins and was raised three days later.

4. Repent for your sins and get baptized in the name of Jesus.

Romans 10:9 (KJV)

⁹That if thou shalt confess with thy mouth the Lord Jesus, and shalt believe in thine heart that God hath raised him from the dead, thou shalt be saved.

To accept Jesus Christ into your heart and live your life to the fullest measure in his kingdom, repeat after me:

Salvation Prayer

Dear Lord, I come to You in the name of Jesus. I acknowledge to You that I am a sinner, and I am sorry for my sins and the life that I have lived; I ask You to forgive me.

I believe that Your only begotten Son, Jesus Christ, died for my sins, and I turn from my sins today.

Your Word says in Romans 10:9 that, "If thou shalt confess with thy mouth the Lord Jesus, and shalt believe in thine heart that God hath raised him from the dead, thou shall be saved."

Right now, I confess Jesus as the

Lord of my life. With all my heart, I believe that God raised Jesus from the dead. This very moment, I accept Jesus Christ as my own personal Lord and Savior; and according to His Word, right now, I am saved.

Thank you Jesus for redeeming me from my sins. I thank you, Jesus, that your grace is enough. Therefore Lord Jesus, transform my life so that I may bring glory and honor to your name.

Thank you Jesus for dying on the cross for me and giving me eternal life. Amen.

Glory to the Lamb of God!
Glory to the Lamb of God!

Thank you, Jesus! It is with great joy that I welcome you into the kingdom of God.

Glory to God!

Luke 15:10 (KJV)

[10]Likewise, I say unto you, there is joy in the presence of the angels of God over one sinner that repenteth.

If you said that prayer, please continue to read this book. This book was written under the influence of the Holy Spirit to enlighten, edify, and educate God's people about His timeless economic plan. The Bible states that God knew us before we were in our mother's womb. God's plan is for us to prosper, and our salvation is the first step.

Romans 10:10 (KJV)

¹⁰For with the heart man believeth unto righteousness; and with the mouth confession is made unto salvation.

What is salvation?

Salvation is the act of saving or protecting from harm, risk, loss, destruction, etc. Theology defines salvation as deliverance from the power and penalty of sin; redemption. Today is your day to change your life, economic situation, belief system, and to be redeemed.

3

Become a Prepared Co-Laborer with God

What does that mean?

It means that you have surrendered your will for God's and are made ready for God to use you.

The Greek word for laborer is "ergates."

It is used 15 times in the New Testament; 11 relate to harvesting, which means a laborer is involved in harvesting.

Luke 10:2 (KJV)

²The harvest truly is great, but the laborers are few."

As a prepared co-laborer with God we are called to be disciples actively involved in the process of evangelizing the lost and establishing the saved.

To be a co-laborer with God we must be bound with God.

"Attached to God"

We must meditate on His Word day and night, always having faith in all of His promises. To be in the presence of God is fullness of joy. I can testify that if you acknowledge God He will direct your path.

"GOD'S GRACE IS SUFFICIENT"

God said to Paul in 2 Corinthians 12:9, *My grace is sufficient for thee.* God will prepare us for the Spiritual and Practical battles that have been foretold in the Bible.

Have you made practical preparation also?

We see all through the Bible that people had to be prepared, and they had to work. James chapter 2 tells us

17

that faith without works is dead. As Believers we often say that God will provide, and that is true. However, taking hold of God's provision requires work; we have to *do* something.

Matthew 17:27 (KJV)

[27]Notwithstanding, lest we should offend them, go thou to the sea, and cast an hook, and take up the fish that first cometh up; and when thou hast opened his mouth, thou shalt find a piece of money: that take, and give unto them for me and thee.

As we can see in this example, Jesus gave instructions to Peter. He told him to go to the sea, cast in a hook and to take the first fish he caught, open its mouth, and there he would find a piece of money. God will provide for our needs, but we have to do our part. Again, James chapter 2 verse 20 states that "Faith without works is dead." We, as children of God, must realize that we too have to work and to not think that everything will be handed to us on a silver platter. If Jesus is our great example and he had to have water to turn into wine and five loaves and two fish to feed the five thousand, we too must use what we have to make provision for ourselves and others. So why do we sometimes have the mentality that we don't have to work hard? Jesus makes a profound statement in the gospel of John.

John 14:12 (KJV)

12Verily, verily, I say unto you, He that believeth on me, the works that I do shall he do also; and greater works than these shall he do; because I go unto my Father.

Let's pray.

Dear God, You said in James 1:5 that, *"If any of you lack wisdom, let him ask of God, that giveth to all men liberally, and upbraideth not; and it shall be given him."* So, Father, we ask that You give us the wisdom to overstand the meaning of this passage in Your Word right now, at this very moment.

The Holy Spirit has revealed to me this day that we are winning in the spiritual realm. God has given us the authority and power to do greater works. The meaning of *greater* is: of an extent, amount, or intensity considerably above the normal or average. The term *works* implies physical or mental effort or activity directed toward the production or accomplishment of something. Now let's put this whole statement together:

12Verily, verily, I say unto you, He that believeth on me, the (physical or mental effort or activity directed toward the production or accomplishment of something) that I do shall he do also; and (that of an extent, amount, or intensity considerably above the normal or average physical or mental effort or activity directed toward the production or accomplishment of something) than these shall he do; because I go unto my Father.

Now that's really an amazing statement for Believers. Jesus is telling us that we have the ability, through faith in God, to defeat the enemy, with his tyranny and oppression, and even stop this New World Order. The answer is yes. Our enemy might employ many carnal weapons such as an army, bioweapons, and the mass media to accomplish his hellish agenda, but

we are assured victory in the Word of
God.

Isaiah 54:17 (KJV)

*[17]No weapon that is formed against
thee shall prosper; and every tongue
that shall rise against thee in
judgment thou shalt condemn. This is
the heritage of the servants of the
LORD, and their righteousness is of
me, saith the LORD.*

Folks, we are already in judgment and every tongue that is rising against us is being condemned in the Spirit.

2 Corinthians 10:4 (KJV)

⁴For the weapons of our warfare are not carnal, but mighty through God to the pulling down of strong holds.

We have to get back to basic reality. We have taken the bailout offered by television and electronic devices for the parenting of our children. Now is the time for a return to simplicity. Whatever happened to Sunday dinners? Backyard gardening? Hugs and family time? These things have been replaced with fast-food meals, mega grocery stores, text messages, and reality TV shows.

Today, technology does more to desensitize us and disconnect us from reality than it does to bring us closer to the way things really are. Our worldview is being formed by the limited information we get on the news. We now live in a world of corporate thugs who have enough money to beat a court case. Our society is driven by money. The term *by-hook-or-crook*—referring to "by whatever means necessary" be it righteous or unrighteous—could be used as a catchphrase for society. Now, there is little to no such thing as business ethnics. The major pharmaceutical companies don't sell cures, only bandages. The enterprises of today are ruthless monopolies.

Do you really want the truth?

They say you can't handle the truth.

Well maybe you can or can't.

Here is the truth.

Money is of zero value. It is a manipulation of one's mind to think otherwise.

Please let me explain:

OK, let's say I have a million dollars in a suitcase and throw it on the ground. Can I talk to the money and say build me a house?

NO! Why is that?

It is because money has no value. An accurate definition of value is worth in usefulness or importance to the possessor. Can you eat money? Some would say I could go to the store and buy food with it. Do you think in a time of a major disaster it would help you? What if you are unable to leave your home—would it be valuable then? In a 2011 Gallup poll, 36% of Americans said they had "very little" or 'no' confidence in U.S. banks. I would estimate that at least 50% of people in the U.S. do have confidence in banks. Well folks, have the banks ever failed? In the last quarter of 1931 alone, more than 1,000 U.S. banks failed as borrowers defaulted and bank assets declined in value. This led to scenes of panic throughout the country, with long lines of customers queuing up before dawn in hopes of withdrawing cash before the banks had no more to pay out. This could be you! There are already lines at the banks sometimes. I spend so much time there sometimes I feel like I work there. Hey, when is payday!

Please don't forever be naïve. Be informed so you can make the right decisions for your family. How about that house I built with a million dollars in a suitcase? Well, the money just blew away. It blew away! I have recognized that it's God's great people who are valuable and not money. We can only serve one master. We must choose: it's either God or money. We have to devalue money, revalue ourselves, and acknowledge that we are the great builders of this land.

Be prepared just like a car is prepared for a flat. Let us become prepared co-laborers with God.

Ephesians 5:15-16 (KJV)

[15]See then that ye walk circumspectly, not as fools, but as wise, [16]Redeeming the time, because the days are evil.

Co-laboring with God is to walk wisely with Him, redeeming the times, and making sure every moment counts with Him because the days ahead are evil. Let your preparation be in divine alignment with the all-sufficient God.

Start Living the Life

2 Corinthians 5:17 (KJV)

[17]Therefore if any man be in Christ, he is a new creature: old things are passed away; behold, all things are become new.

We as Believers have to adopt this way of thinking to fulfill God's plan for our lives. Our thoughts create our experiences and our experiences create our circumstances.

Shocking News!!!

Thinking negatively will produce negative results. Have you ever thought something really negative and saw what you had been thinking come to pass? This is because our thoughts contribute to our feelings. For example, seeing a commercial on TV showing snow, someone ice-skating, or a cold event can make us feel cold. Who hasn't seen a scrumptious-looking meal in a commercial and felt hungry immediately afterward?

The reason this happens is because our minds don't know real from imagination. Let's see what the Bible says about how and what we should think. Thinking positive is sure to create positive results and environments. Start saying positive affirmations, which are just positive statements.

Philippians 4:8 (KJV)

⁸Finally, brethren, whatsoever things are true, whatsoever things are honest, whatsoever things are just, whatsoever things are pure, whatsoever things are lovely, whatsoever things are of good report; if there be any virtue, and if there be any praise, think on these things.

OUR THOUGHTS AND WORDS HAVE POWER!!!

Proverbs 18:21 (KJV)

21 Death and life are in the power of the tongue: and they that love it shall eat the fruit thereof.

Genesis 1:3 (KJV)

3 And God said, Let there be light: and there was light.

As we can see in the scriptures above, our words have the power and ability to create. Because of this "Word power" we have to be really careful about what we speak. If you are new to this way of thinking it may become a battle in the mind. They say that you can't teach an old dog new tricks, but in this case it's a must so that we can survive. Old things must pass away to get to a new, more positive you.

Relationships that hinder our development must be abandoned so they can't prevent our success. They say misery loves company. The crabs in a bucket scenario demonstrates why this is so. As the crab is making its way to the top and begins to free itself, another crab pulls it down. In perspective, our friends, family, and associates may be hindering our growth by being unsupportive, selfish, controlling, and faithless. Some people call this behavior "hating." I would call this behavior a form of witchcraft. I say this because if our words have power, speaking and acting negatively is sure to cause negative results.

5

Health Is Wealth

EAT 85

Eat 85 is a concept that I thought of years ago. Eat 85 suggests that we should eat healthy at least 85% of the time.

Nothing has as sizable of an impact on our health as the food we choose to eat. A diet rich in vegetables, whole grains, legumes, fish, and fruit can prevent and even reverse most of the diseases that devastate our world today. The positive news is that farm-fresh, seasonal produce happens to be some of the most delightful food on the earth.

Unfortunately, our society does not make it easy to obtain foods that are healthy and safe to eat. Our typical grocery store is filled with processed, packaged junk foods that are made with genetically modified organisms or GMOs (usually corn and soybeans). Even the produce section is populated with cloned foods shipped from halfway around the world.

Quit Smoking! Smoking is committing a slow suicide.

Most people know that smoking can cause lung cancer, but it can also cause many other cancers and illnesses.

Cigarettes contain more than 4,000 chemical compounds and at least 400 toxic substances.

When you inhale, a cigarette burns at 700°C at the tip and around 60°C in the core. This heat breaks down the tobacco to produce various toxins.

As a cigarette burns, the residues are concentrated towards the butt.

The products that are most damaging are:

1. Tar – a carcinogen (substance that causes cancer)
2. Nicotine – an addictive substance that increases cholesterol levels in your body
3. Carbon monoxide – a gas that reduces oxygen in the body
4. Components of the gas and particulate phases cause chronic obstructive pulmonary disorder (COPD).

The damage caused by smoking is influenced by:

1. The number of cigarettes smoked
2. Whether or not the cigarette has a filter
3. How the tobacco was prepared.

Did you know smoking affects how long you live!

Research has shown that smoking reduces life expectancy by seven to eight years.

Smoking raises blood pressure, which can cause hypertension (high blood pressure) – a risk factor for heart attacks and strokes. Couples who smoke are more likely to have fertility problems than couples who are non-smokers.

For men in their 30s and 40s, smoking increases the risk of erectile dysfunction (ED) by about 50%.

Erection can't occur unless blood can flow freely into the penis, so these blood vessels have to be in great condition.

Smoking can damage the blood vessels and cause them to degenerate. Nicotine narrows the arteries that lead to the penis, reducing blood flow and the pressure of blood in the penis.

This narrowing effect will increase over time, so if you don't have problems now, things could change later.

The deciding factors: I would base a decision to stop smoking on my family and my health. You make the choice for you.

Exercise

Exercise can help maintain weight loss or help prevent excess weight gain. When you engage in physical activity, your body burns calories. We don't have to do long workouts in the gym or run miles to see results in our body. We simply must change our routine. Like parking at the end of a mall parking lot instead of looking for an "up-front" parking spot, or even using a good jump rope.

Exercise can help prevent or help combat health conditions and diseases. Regular physical activity can help prevent or manage different health problems. Also, exercise helps improve our moods. Working out at the gym or taking a walk in the park can help us relax. Studies show physical activity stimulates various brain chemicals that may leave you feeling happier and more relaxed. Regular exercise is sure to boost confidence and improve our self-esteem. Exercising regularly can improve your muscle strength and boost endurance. Physical activity delivers oxygen and key nutrients to our tissues and helps fuel our cardiovascular system, making it more efficient. When our lungs and heart work more efficiently we have more energy.

So do we really need that energy drink?

6

End Time Prophecy

In a vision God spoke to me…

God told me to write this book and compile it with information that will help us to be prepared for coming events. I wanted to make it an average-size book, but the Holy Spirit inspired me to make it pocket size. The reason, I believe, is so it could be easily stored on the go, making it possible to be hidden from an enemy.

The prediction is that the rulers of this world will outlaw and band *digital versatile discs (known as DVDs), which* are high-density videodiscs that store large amounts of data as well as high-resolution audio-visual material. Also, *compact* discs, or CDs for short, are optical discs used to store digital data. They were originally developed to store and play back sound recordings only, but the format was later adapted for storage of data.

The reason is simple. *Data* is information that has been translated into a form that is more convenient to move or process. In the event that the cable, radio, and Internet shut down, these discs can be used as a type of Underground Railroad, so to speak, to move information like during the time of slavery in America.

A simple disc can be duplicated an infinite number of times and be watched by a massive number of people. The Internet digital technology can be cut off in just a zap in accordance with executive orders.

To combat this effort, we must store blank DVD, CD, and CD/DVD burners and players, and keep data DVDs and CDs with information on what to do in a time of crisis to send as messages.

Prayers for Spiritual Battles

Ephesians 6:12 (KJV)

12For we wrestle not against flesh and blood, but against principalities, against powers, against the rulers of the darkness of this world, against spiritual wickedness in high places.

2 Corinthians 10:4 (KJV)

4For the weapons of our warfare are not carnal, but mighty through God to the pulling down of strong holds.

In 1 Thessalonians 5:17, the Bible tells us to pray without ceasing.

In this current world climate, we must pray to defend our homeland. For carnal weapons are useless against spiritual battles.

If a government is against the people, the only way we can truly win is to pray. **How can we really fight a militarized government? They run the sky, land, and sea. They have the latest weaponry.** *The clue to winning this type of battle is evident. Over 50 years ago,* the U.S. Supreme Court issued two bans on prayer in public schools. The first ban came in 1962 and the second was issued in 1963.

God's people please listen. We have Word power. Our words have power when we pray.

Prayer Changes Things on the Earth.

The enemy knows that's the only way we can beat him.

Jesus said to the devil in Matthew 4:4 *Man shall not live by bread alone, but by every word that proceedeth out of the mouth of God.* We, as Believers in Christ, have to pray the Word of God without ceasing. In addition to that, we must pray the Scripture and not just empty words. God obligates Himself to respond to His words.

Matthew 6:7-13 (KJV)

7But when ye pray, use not vain repetitions, as the heathen do: for they think that they shall be heard for their much speaking.

8Be not ye therefore like unto them: for your Father knoweth what things ye have need of, before ye ask him.

9After this manner therefore pray ye: Our Father which art in heaven, Hallowed be thy name.

10Thy kingdom come, Thy will be done in earth, as it is in heaven.

11Give us this day our daily bread.

¹² And forgive us our debts, as we forgive our debtors.

¹³ And lead us not into temptation, but deliver us from evil: For thine is the kingdom, and the power, and the glory, forever. Amen.

God has given us this great pattern for prayer.

1. First, we acknowledge Him.
2. We ask that His will be done.
3. We should pray that He feed us and supply our daily needs.
4. We pray for forgiveness for ourselves and forgive others.
5. We ask that God would provide a way to escape when we are tempted and that He would protect us from evil.

6. And finally, an acknowledgment of who He is and the power He has.

When we pray, we should think deeply about and remind God of His Word in prayer. Most of us have either heard the words or said to our parents, "But you said…," when asking them for things. We should remember that God is our Father and we should speak with Him accordingly.

We are about to learn to use the Word of God as a weapon for Spiritual Self-Defense.

EVERYDAY PRAYER

Dear Heavenly Father, in the name of Jesus, I put on the whole armor of God, that I may be able to stand against the wiles of the devil. For I wrestle not against flesh and blood, but against principalities, powers, the rulers of the darkness of this world, and against spiritual wickedness in high places.

Therefore, I stand firmly in this evil day having my loins gird about with truth. I am able and mighty through You, my God, to pull down strongholds.

I am covered with the breastplate of righteousness, which is faith and

love. My feet are shod with the
preparation of the Gospel of peace.
God, I thank You that I am forever in
Your presence because there I
experience the fullness of joy. I will
pursue peace with all humanity.

I use the shield of faith now to
quench all the fiery darts of the
wicked. My head is covered with the
helmet of salvation. I have the Word
of God, which is the sword of the
Spirit. I am victorious in all trials,
temptations, and tests. I thank You
that greater is He that is in me than
he that is in the world. In the name of
Jesus Christ I plead the blood of
Jesus over this prayer. Amen.

HEALING PRAYER

Father God, I come boldly to the throne of grace to obtain Your great mercy. I believe according to 1 Peter 2:24 that by Jesus Christ's stripes I am healed. Therefore, I receive healing now. The Word says Jesus himself took our infirmities and bore our sicknesses. I am redeemed from the curse of sickness and refuse to tolerate its symptoms.

Satan, you are bound from operating against me in any way. I am God's property. I abide in the shadow of the Most High, whose power no foe can withstand.

I dwell in the secret place of the
Most High. Your angels encamp
around me and deliver me from every
evil work. No plague or calamity
shall come near my dwelling. The
Word of God abides in me. I am
whole in body, mind, and spirit. The
Spirit of life operates in me and
makes me free from the law of sin
and death.

I thank You Father that Your
Word, which will not return to You
void but will accomplish what it says
it will. I thank You for my healing in
the name of Your Son, Jesus Christ. I
plead the blood of Jesus. Amen.

PROSPERITY PRAYER

Hallelujah! Thank You, Holy Father. I come to You in the name of your Son, Jesus. I thank You for giving your Son Jesus so that my family and I may have prosperity. I confess Your Word over my finances today.

Satan, I bind you from my finances, according to Matthew 18:18 and loose you from your assignment against me in the name of Jesus.

In the name of Jesus all my needs are met according to Philippians 4:19. I believe that because I have given tithes and offerings to further

Your cause, gifts will be given to me, good measure, pressed down, shaken together and running over. They will be poured into my bosom. For with the measure I deal out, it will be measured back to me.

I am delivered from the authority of darkness and poverty into the kingdom of Jesus Christ. I am Your child. Father, I thank You for providing for my every need. I believe that I receive all that I ask in this prayer and that You look over your Word to perform it and it will not return to You void. I am in right standing to receive Your blessing, protection, and provision. I walk in Your perfect wisdom and love. Father you said in Your Word if any of you lack wisdom ask. Therefore, I ask for the wisdom of God for my finances. Father give me the wisdom to manage my resources with excellence. Lord, give me the heart of a giver that I may be a blessing on the earth and to Your people.

Father, I thank You that Your ministering spirits are now free to minister to me and bring in the necessary finances.

God, You are a very present help in my time of need. You alone are able to make all grace abound. I declare every favor and earthly blessing to come to me now in abundance. In the name of Jesus Christ I pray pleading the blood. Amen.

Tips and Facts to Become More Prepared in Times of Crisis

Emergency Preparedness. Have an emergency food supply. No one knows when a natural disaster (earthquake, fire, or flood) may strike and access to your local food store may not be an option.

Be Prepared to Help Others. A food supply can be used to help your friends, neighbors, family members, or anyone else in need.

Psalm 112:5 (KJV)

⁵A good man sheweth favour, and lendeth: he will guide his affairs with discretion.

Storms and Weather. Catastrophic events, as we have seen, can make food impossible to transport, destroy crops, and isolate people from supplies. Serious American crop failures are creating shortages of food to be processed into supplies for people to store, even though you may not have seen these shortages yet in the grocery stores.

Global Warming. Whether real or fabricated, the concept of "Global Warming" will likely be used for

taxation of farmers, to control
fertilization of crops, and control
how much and what foods we can
buy. Legislation has been passed in
certain areas that prevent people
from gardening and mandate what
farmers can grow and how to grow it.
To plant gardens for hard times is
good if you can, but the majority of
our population has no place or time
to plant them.

Inflation. One in five Americans
presently worry about getting food
daily. Runaway inflation in Germany
and Argentina should serve as a
warning for us. They followed the
same inflationary path that the
United States is presently on and the
price of a loaf of bread, milk, and

even water have tripled like gas prices.

Other reasons you should be prepared:

• Political anarchy or revolution

• Racial strife or civil war

• Spread of disease such as a plague or bird flu pandemic

• Power grid failure

• Electromagnetic pulse event

An electromagnetic pulse (EMP), also sometimes called a transient electromagnetic disturbance, is a short burst of electromagnetic energy. Such a pulse's origination may be a natural occurrence or man-made and can occur as a radiated, electric, or magnetic field or a conducted electric current, depending on the source.

EMP interference is generally disruptive or damaging to electronic equipment, and at higher energy levels a powerful EMP event such as a lightning strike can damage physical objects such as buildings and aircraft structures. The management of EMP effects is an important branch of electromagnetic compatibility (EMC) engineering. Weapons have been developed to deliver the damaging effects of high-energy EMP.

To prepare for the worst you need a good plan. Why are most people so against doing basic preparations that could be the difference on how they survive or *whether* they survive?

Well, 55% of Americans believe that the government will come to their aid in times of crisis. I just pray that there aren't more hurricanes like Katrina or Harvey. You know what happened with those.

Your list of supplies and/or preparations should include:

Water – We can't survive a week without this. (We should also know how to treat and sterilize water supplies.)

Food Storage

Food Preparation

Gardening by Seed

Hygiene/Sanitation Supplies

Hunting/Fishing/Trapping

Power/Lighting/Batteries

Fuels

Firefighting

First Aid/Minor Surgery

Nuclear Defense

Biological Warfare Defense

Tactical Living

Security-General

Security-Firearms

Communications/Monitoring

Tools

Sundries (items of little value)

Survival Bookshelf

Barter and charity

Start to work with like-minded people who share your views, goals, and values.

We need to be prepared. The Bible teaches us that God's people perish for the lack of knowledge. If you are reading this book, consider this an exhortation for what to do now given the state of our land as well as a spiritual guide to help our minds, bodies, and souls.

Terms and Definitions You Need to Know

1. **Agenda 21** – a non-binding and voluntarily implemented action plan of the United Nations (UN) related to sustainable development. It was a core work product from the United Nations Conference on Environment and Development. Succinctly, Agenda 21 is a comprehensive blueprint of action to be taken globally, nationally, and locally by organizations of the UN,

governments, and major groups in every area in which humans directly affect the environment. The "21" in Agenda 21 refers to 21st Century.

2. **Alkaline Water** – water that contains appreciable amounts of the bicarbonates of calcium, lithium, potassium, or sodium.

3. **Authoritarian** – favoring complete obedience or subjection to authority as opposed to individual freedom: authoritarian principles; authoritarian attitudes. May pertain to a governmental or political system, principle, or practice in which individual freedom is held as completely subordinate to the power or authority of the state, centered either on one person or a small

group that is not constitutionally accountable to the people. Also exercising complete or almost complete control over the will of another or of others: an authoritarian parent.

4. **Bondage** – slavery or involuntary servitude; serfdom. The state of being bound by or subjected to some external power or control. The state or practice of being physically restrained, as by being tied up, chained, or put in handcuffs.

5. **Compound Interest** – *Interest* that accrues on the initial principal and the accumulated *interest* of a principal deposit, loan, or debt.

6. **Council on Foreign Relations (CFR)** – an American nonprofit,

nonpartisan membership organization, publisher, and think tank specializing in U.S. foreign policy and international affairs. Founded in 1921 and headquartered at 58 East 68th Street in New York City, with an additional office in Washington, D.C., the CFR is considered to be the nation's "most influential foreign-policy think tank."

7. **Democide** – systematic slaughter of a subject population by its government. "The murder of any person or people by a government, including genocide, politicide, and mass murder."

8. **Disruptive Technology** – an innovation that helps create a new

market and value network, and eventually goes on to disrupt an existing market and value network, displacing an earlier technology. Example of disruptive technologies could be a cure for a disease or a car that runs without gas. It would put pharmaceutical and oil companies out of business instantly.

9. **Drone** – an unmanned aerial vehicle (**UAV**); an aircraft without a human pilot onboard. Its flight is either controlled autonomously by computers in the vehicle, or under the remote control of a navigator, or pilot on the ground or in another vehicle.

10. **Eugenics** – the study of or belief in the possibility of improving the

qualities of the human species or a
human population, especially by
such means as discouraging
reproduction by persons having
genetic defects or presumed to have
inheritable undesirable traits or
encouraging reproduction by persons
presumed to have inheritable
desirable traits.

11. **Executive Order** – a rule or order
issued by the president to an
executive branch of the government
and having the force of law. It is a
fact that a complete dictatorship can
be imposed upon the people at any
time, simply by the president
declaring a national emergency.

12. **Fiat Currency** – money that derives
its value from government

regulation or law; the initial value of fiat money is established by governmental decree. The history of fiat money has been one of failure. In fact, EVERY fiat currency since the Romans first began the practice in the first century has ended in devaluation and eventual collapse, of not only the currency but of the economy that housed the fiat currency as well.

13. **Fractional Banking** – a banking system in which only a fraction of bank deposits are backed by actual cash-on-hand and are available for withdrawal. Many U.S. banks were forced to shut down during the Great Depression because

so many people attempted to withdraw assets at the same time.

14. **Freedom** – the state of being free or at liberty rather than in confinement or under physical restraint; exemption from external control, interference, regulation, political or national independence personal liberty, as opposed to bondage or slavery, etc.

15. **Genocide** – the deliberate and systematic destruction, in whole or in part, of an ethnic, racial, religious, or national group.

16. **Globalist** – a person who advocates the interpretation or planning of economic and foreign policy in relation to events and developments throughout the world.

17. **GMO** – genetically modified organism; found in most food, it's an organism whose genetic material has been altered using genetic engineering techniques.

18. **Homeland Security** – the United States Department of Homeland Security, the body responsible for dealing with terrorist threats on American soil.

19. **Hybrid Seed** – a seed produced by artificially cross-pollinated plants. Hybrid seed cannot be saved, as the seed from the first generation of hybrid plants does not reliably produce true copies; therefore, new seed must be purchased for each planting.

20. **Hydrogen Fluoride** – hydrogen fluoride is regulated as a hazardous pollutant in emissions from chemical plants and has been linked to respiratory illness.

21. **Illuminati** – (plural of Latin *illuminatus*, "enlightened") a name given to several groups, both real (historical) and fictitious. Historically, the name refers to the Bavarian Illuminati, an Enlightenment-era secret society founded on May 1, 1776. In more modern contexts the name refers to a purported conspiratorial organization, which is alleged to mastermind events and control world affairs through governments

and corporations to establish a New World Order.

22. **International Monetary Fund (IMF)** – an international organization that was created on July 22, 1944 at the Bretton Woods Conference and came into existence on December 27, 1945 when 29 countries signed the Articles of Agreement. It originally had 45 members. The IMF's stated goal was to stabilize exchange rates and assist the reconstruction of the world's international payment system post-World War II. Countries contribute money to a pool through a quota system from which countries with payment imbalances can borrow funds temporarily. The

organization's stated objectives are to promote international economic cooperation, international trade, employment, and exchange rate stability by making financial resources available to member countries to meet the balance of payments needs. Its headquarters is in Washington, D.C.

23. **Liberty** – freedom from arbitrary or despotic government or control, or from external or foreign rule; independence. Freedom from control, interference, obligation, restriction, hampering conditions, etc.; power or right of doing, thinking, speaking, etc., according to choice. Freedom from captivity, confinement, or physical restraint.

24. Martial Law – the imposition of military rule by military authorities over designated regions on an emergency basis—(usually) only temporary—when the civilian government or civilian authorities fail to function effectively (e.g., maintain order and security, and provide essential services), when there are extensive riots and protests, or when the disobedience of the law becomes widespread. In most cases, military forces are deployed to subdue the crowds, to secure government buildings and key or sensitive locations, and to maintain order. Generally, military personnel replace civil authorities and perform some or all of their functions.

Martial law can be used by governments to enforce their rule over the public. Typically, the imposition of martial law accompanies curfews, the suspension of civil law, civil rights, habeas corpus, and the application or extension of military law or military justice to civilians. Civilians defying martial law may be subjected to military tribunal (court martial).

25. **Meltdown** – the melting of a significant portion of a nuclear-reactor core due to inadequate cooling of the fuel elements, a condition that could lead to the escape of radiation.

26. **Minion** – a follower devoted to serve his/her master relentlessly. An

obsequious follower or dependent; a sycophant.

27. **Monopoly** – exclusive control of a commodity or service in a particular market, or a control that makes possible the manipulation of prices. The exclusive possession or control of something.

28. **Nanotechnology** – (sometimes shortened to "**nanotech**") the manipulation of matter on an atomic and molecular scale. Nanotechnology may be able to create many new materials and devices with a vast range of applications, such as in medicine, electronics, biomaterials, and energy production. On the other hand, nanotechnology raises many of the

same issues as any new technology, including concerns about the toxicity and environmental impact of nanomaterials, and their potential effects on global economics as well as speculation about various doomsday scenarios.

29. **New World Order** – a worldwide conspiracy being orchestrated by an extremely powerful and influential group of genetically related individuals (at least at the highest echelons) who include many of the world's wealthiest people, top political leaders, and corporate elite, whose goal is to create a One World (fascist) Government, stripped of nationalistic and regional boundaries, that is obedient to their

agenda. Their intention is to effect complete and total control over every human being on the planet and to dramatically reduce the world's population by 5.5 billion people.

30. **Paramilitary** – an organization operating as, in place of, or as a supplement to, a regular military force.

31. **Patriot** – a person who loves, supports, and defends his or her country and its interests with devotion. A person who regards himself or herself as a defender, especially of individual rights, against presumed interference by the federal government. A person who vigorously supports his country and its ways of life.

32. Prison Industrial Complex (PIC) –
a term used to attribute the rapid
expansion of the U.S. inmate
population to the political influence
of private prison companies and
businesses that supply goods and
services to government prison
agencies. The United States has
the highest documented
incarceration rate in the world,
surpassing China, North Korea, and
Russia. The United States spends
more on prisons and incarcerates
more people than any other
industrialized country in the world.
Over 5 million are in prison, on
parole or probation, or are
incarcerated in INS detention
centers. Between 1971 and 1992,

public spending on prisons alone jumped from $2.3 billion to $31.2 billion. Altogether, corrections' spending is growing at a faster rate than Medicaid, higher education, and Aid to Families with Dependent Children. In 1995, prison building expenditures jumped by $926 million while university construction dropped by $954 million. Prisons soak up over $32 billion while generating billions of dollars in profit for big business. Corporations are receiving a growing proportion of our tax dollars to operate private prisons and provide services. Between 1987 and 1996, the number of inmates in private prisons jumped from 3,122 to 78,000. The prison industry generates an estimated $40 billion a year.

33. **Privatism** – a generic term generally describing any belief that people have a right to the private ownership of certain things.

34. **Propaganda** – a message designed to persuade its intended audience to think and behave in a certain manner.

35. **Publicity Stunt** – a planned event designed to attract the public's attention to the event's organizers or their cause. Publicity stunts can be professionally organized or set up by amateurs.

36. **Sanction** – authoritative permission or approval, as for an action.

Something that gives binding force, as to an oath, rule of conduct, etc.

37. **Social Engineering** – the manipulation of the social position and function of individuals in order to manage change in a society.

38. **Takeover** – the act of seizing, appropriating, or arrogating authority, control, management, etc.

39. **Thimerosal** – the preservative of choice for vaccine manufacturers. Thimerosal contains 49.6% mercury by weight and is metabolized or degraded into ethyl mercury and thiosalicylate. The Department of Defense classifies mercury as a hazardous material that could cause death if swallowed, inhaled, or absorbed through the skin. Studies

indicate that mercury tends to accumulate in the brains of primates and other animals after they are injected with vaccines. Mercury poisoning has been linked to cardiovascular disease, autism, seizures, mental retardation, hyperactivity, dyslexia, and many other nervous system conditions. That's why the FDA rigorously limits exposure to mercury in foods and drugs. Some common sources of mercury include dental amalgam fillings, various vaccines, and certain fish contaminated by polluted ocean waters.

40. **TSA (Transportation Security Administration)** – an agency established in 2001 to safeguard United States transportation systems and ensure safe air travel.

41. **Tyranny** – cruel and oppressive government or rule.

42. **Tyrant** – a sovereign or other ruler who uses power oppressively or unjustly. Any person in a position of authority who exercises power oppressively or despotically. A tyrannical or compulsory influence.

43. **Whistleblower** – a person who informs on another or makes public disclosure of corruption or wrongdoing; an informant who exposes wrongdoing within an organization in the hope of stopping it.